COLOR IN ARCHITECTURAL ILLUSTRATION

COLOR IN ARCHITECTURAL ILLUSTRATION

RICHARD ROCHON AND HAROLD LINTON

VNR VAN NOSTRAND REINHOLD
New York

To Ben

Full-page Illustrations

Frontispiece, Woodbridge Office Building, Smith, Hinchman & Grylls Associates, Inc.
Fig. 17, Page 22, Visual Awareness, *Collection of Richard Rochon.*
Fig. 39, Page 44, Atwater Landing, Schervish, Vogel, Merz, P.C.
Fig. 59, Page 70, Crescent Centre—Phase I, Skidmore Owings & Merrill, Architects/Engineers.
Fig. 81, Page 98, Houston Street Mural, Collection of Richard Rochon.

Copyright © 1989 by Richard Rochon and Harold Linton

Library of Congress Catalog Card Number 88-3649

ISBN 0-442-27672-9

Printed in Hong Kong

Designed by Richard Rochon

Van Nostrand Reinhold
115 Fifth Avenue
New York, New York 10003

Van Nostrand Reinhold Company Limited
Molly Millars Lane
Wokingham, Berkshire RG11 2PY, England

Van Nostrand Reinhold
480 La Trobe Street
Melbourne, Victoria 3000, Australia

Macmillan of Canada
Division of Canada Publishing Corporation
164 Commander Boulevard
Agincourt, Ontario MIS 3C7, Canada

16 15 14 13 12 11 10 9 8 7 6 5 4 3 2 1

Library of Congress Cataloging-in-Publication Data

Rochon, Richard.
    Color in architectural illustration/Richard Rochon and Harold Linton.

    p.   cm.
    Bibliography: p.
    Includes index.
    ISBN 0-442-27672-9
    1. Architectural drawing—Great Britain.   2. Color in art.
I. Linton, Harold.   II. Title.
NA2706.G7R63 1989
720′.28′40942—dc19   88-3649
                                                      CIP

CONTENTS

FOREWORD

This book deals with an aspect of architectural illustration that is timely, informative, powerful, and highly elusive. The extensive amount of investigation and speculation about the phenomenon of color itself would suggest the difficulty of understanding fully its nature or mastering its application. The relatively modest scope of this work, however, is to record some observations and examples of effective color use in the illustration of designed form and to provide insight—and perhaps inspiration—for anyone interested in architecture and its representation.

The subject of color in the representation of architecture is particularly timely now that architecture is becoming dramatically polychromatic. A major function of architectural illustration has always been to communicate the intent of the designer through faithful representation of the designed form, whether by realistic (visual) or schematic (diagrammatic) means. The recent "modern" era of architectural design was characterized by a preference for materials and finishes that tended to be neutral or subtle in chroma. The use of black, white, gray, and natural beige—with an occasional primary color as accent—seemed to be the canon. This led naturally to the achromatic representation of architecture, since the chromatic intent or statement was usually absent. (Conversely, it might be argued that the habit of producing black-and-white drawings led to the building of monochromatic architecture.) At any rate, with the recent advent of more strongly and integrally chromatic buildings, there follows the challenge to visualize and represent them as accurately as possible.

The aspect of color in graphic representation carries an enormous capacity to distinguish and inform. Although the basic building block of visual description in two dimensions is value or tone (lightness and darkness), the addition of color substantially enhances the black-and-white image. Whereas tonal range is sometimes quantified in ten or twenty gradations (those numbers can be greatly amplified by variations in context), hue and chroma variations number in the millions, as any computer graphics technician is quick to point out. Since nonlinear contour definition in graphic representation depends on the differentiation among contiguous areas, the advantage of an extensive palette is obvious. Our ability to use, or even distinguish among, such astronomical numbers of choices is limited by perception and technical considerations, but certainly much more graphic information can be carried by a chromatically varied image than by its achromatic counterpart. The examples of my work included in this book demonstrate the disparity in information imparted.

Color in illustration has the capacity to inform, but its greatest advantage probably lies in its power to inspire. Because of the visceral and subjective nature of color, it is a mighty tool of persuasion. Skillful and sensitive use of color in an illustration can convince and persuade a client (one function of any architectural presentation), whereas a badly handled or inappropriate color application can irretrievably offend or repel the same client, making further progress on the project difficult or impossible. This repulsion may be subliminal, and the client may therefore be unable to separate his or her rejection of the colors from the more substantial aspects of the design. It should be noted that there are two realms of color design—the *designer's* selection of colors and the *illustrator's* representation of that selection. When a designer illustrates his or her own work, or when a designer and illustrator work together, the representation of color in an illustration can inform and modify the selection of color made during the design process.

In spite of many efforts to codify, standardize, and formulate the selection and application of color, its most effective use remains elusive and requires a great deal of subtlety, judgment, experience, and artistic talent. It seems that the best examples of color illustration usually break at least some of the standard rules. Complicating the application of color further are the various ways different people perceive the same color and the various ways color is perceived by the same person when the context changes. A material color in winter light looks different from the same one in summer, and similar inconsistencies occur from sun to shade, day to night, and a dozen other such variations in context. It is well known that the perception of a single color can shift dramatically by placing it next to another color. These shifts become more complex as the numbers of interacting colors increase. The effective use of color is also complicated by reproduction limitations of fidelity and consistency—not to mention cost. Even if the difficult task of translating a projected "reality" into a color image that communicates that sense of reality were achieved, the subtle distinctions of the original image might elude the printed page.

Given the opportunities and difficulties presented by the use of color in architectural description, this book, prepared by a highly skilled perspectivist and a teaching artist of note, should be on the desk of every design professional and student concerned with the effective representation of architecture.

Paul Stevenson Oles

PREFACE

Color in architectural illustration has long enriched, enlivened, and influenced the design of buildings. During the nineteenth and early twentieth centuries, architectural perspective drawing and painting thrived and prospered in Britain to a much greater extent than in most other countries. Architectural representation achieved considerable virtuosity and brilliance while reflecting qualities that distinguished the character of British buildings, with emphasis on texture, color, the nature of site and place, scale and detail, and the pictorial qualities of the romantic and the picturesque. We are grateful to Jill Lever of the Drawings Collection of the Royal Institute of British Architects for her introduction, "Color in English Architectural Drawings," which explores the legacy of color in architectural illustration from the twelfth to the early twentieth centuries, particularly in Britain. Many insights come to light in the beautiful illustrations gathered from the Drawings Collection of the Royal Institute of British Architects, the Sir John Soane Museum, the Bodleian Library, and the Public Record Office.

A distinction between a drawing prepared in advance of an executed structure or as a representation of a building that already exists is vital to an understanding of the role of the architectural illustrator and the skills used to represent a three-dimensional concept. As Raymond Myerscough-Walker expressed in his book, *The Perspectivist*, "The perspective as the drawing of a project not yet built is one of the few possibilities left to the three-dimensional painter with which the camera cannot possibly compete." Although there are several technical systems for establishing the perspective view from plan and elevation drawings, the final impression is influenced by an illustrator's skill, honesty, and vision, which are informed by a knowledge of the way viewers perceive color, light, form, and space and by an understanding of how the structure should look. With the current interest in and return to ornament and detail in architecture, the collaboration between the spheres of art and architecture has intensified and has challenged the architectural illustrator to express graphically the effects of a visually enriched built environment.

Today, the three-dimensional graphic illustration along with architectural models, video technology, and computer graphics are all essential tools used by architects to transform a design into a building. The preparation of perspective illustrations in all forms of pictorial refinement, including computer-generated images in line and tone, has intensified. The three-dimensional graphic is a necessary communication link between the architect and an often uncomprehending public. It offers visual support and documentation to the architect through various stages of design development and facilitates the client's understanding of a concept through its various stages of approval.

The purpose of this book is threefold: to present a historical survey of the development and brilliance of color in English architectural drawing; to relate significant precedents in architectural illustration and the fine arts to a discussion of planning concepts and the visual properties of color for perspective illustrations and renderings; and to relate these aspects to a portfolio of work by accomplished, contemporary illustrators, whose comments regarding color methodologies in architectural illustration and design accompany their work. The discussions and illustrations included provide the reader with insight into the principles that unite color, light, form, and space in the illustration process.

The images beginning with figure 23 in Parts One through Four have been created by Richard Rochon. They have been selected to demonstrate concepts in color illustration and sometimes represent details of larger illustrations. Each detail of a larger work is indicated as such in the figure caption and is often accompanied by a view of the full-color illustration. We would like to extend our acknowledgment and appreciation to Paul Stevenson Oles; Henry Matthews, Curator of Exhibitions and Collections of the Muskegon Museum of Art; contributors to the portfolio section; Annette, Joanne, and Theresa Rochon, for help in assembly and layout design; Carol Kaffenberger and Nadyne Linton for support and advice; Wendy Lochner and Donna Rossler, our editors; The Ford Foundation; The Avery Architecture Library of Columbia University; I. M. Pei and Partners, Architects and Planners; J. Henderson Barr; Helmut Jacoby; Scott Sutton Photographic; The Architectural League of New York; Rockefeller Center; our colleagues at the School of Architecture, Lawrence Institute of Technology; Mike Hoogerhyde, for his assistance with graphic design; and all of the architects who granted permission to reproduce illustrations of their works and whose names are listed following the portfolio section in the book.

INTRODUCTION

COLOR IN ENGLISH ARCHITECTURAL DRAWINGS

Jill Lever

The history of color in architectural drawings probably has its beginnings in the decorated letters of illuminated manuscripts. The use of color (commonly powdered colors dissolved in water bound with egg white or gum, according to the color used, and painted in several layers on vellum) was decorative rather than realistic, for no attention was paid to the actual color of the objects illustrated. Some tenth-century Anglo-Saxon manuscripts show towers, pinnacles, arcading, capitals, and other architectural details as part of a decorative design, but it is a Norman illuminated manuscript of about 1170 that comes nearest to a conventional architect's drawing. Though it illustrates the temple of Ezekiel's vision described in the Bible, the section is very like that of a contemporary Norman castle (fig. 2).

2. Richard of St. Victor. Commentary on the vision of Ezekiel, c. 1170. Illumination on parchment (9″ × 6⅛″ sheet). Oxford, Bodleian Library.

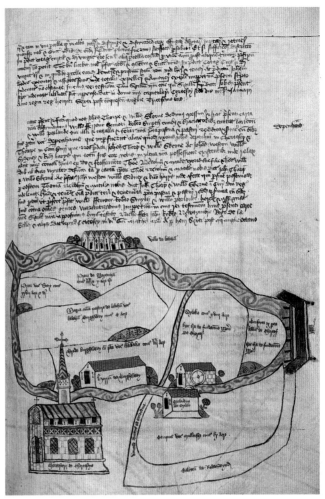

3. Plan on the demesne lands of the Benedictine Abbey of Chertsey, c. 1432. Pen and watercolor (approx. 9¾″ × 6½″). Public Record Office.

The mapmakers of the late Middle Ages adopted the technique of the illuminator (or limner), decorating capital letters and filling spare spaces with vividly colored ornament. At the same time, they employed color in a functional way: from the thirteenth century, seas, lakes, and rivers are colored blue (or green); woodlands are shown in a dark green and brown; and red is used for roads. Buildings and settlements, at first shown in primitive perspective, have roofs colored red to represent tiles; later, when drawn in plan, tile-red was still used for towns and villages (fig. 3). The convention in mapmaking of taking color from nature is still used seven centuries later. Survey drawings of estates, and survey or design drawings prepared by military engineers for fortifications, used the same color conventions, and during the seventeenth century, prospects, or bird's-eye perspectives, were introduced.

Though the total number of European Gothic architectural drawings that survive amounts to perhaps four or five thousand, few of these are English. Color was rarely used, but a late example shows a design for a tower with turrets drawn nearly in pure elevation and with the string courses and cornice in perspective. The medium is brown ink with transparent washes of browns, gray, pink, mauve, and gray-blue on parchment. There seems to be no logic in the use of color for the windows, unless color indicates function—the central windows, washed pink with mauve heads, light the principal rooms and are distinguished from the windows to the stairs and lesser rooms (fig. 4). The purpose of the green wash, hatched and cross-

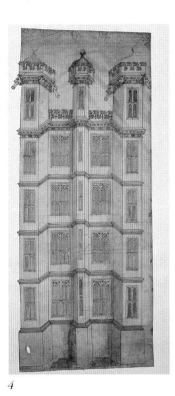

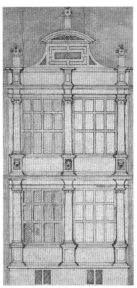

6

4

5

4. Design for a tower with turrets, c. 1500. Brown pen and colored washes on parchment (19¹/₈″ × 7⁷/₈″). Drawings Collection of the Royal Institute of British Architects.

5. Robert Smythson (c. 1535–1614). Design for a two-story bay window, c. 1568–72. Pen with green, brown, and faded pink washes (14¹/₈″ × 7¹/₈″). Drawings Collections of the Royal Institute of British Architects.

6. John Talman (1677–1726). Design for the interior of a room in a house near Hampton Court Palace, c. 1700. Brown pen and watercolor (11⁵/₈″ × 18¹/₂″). Drawings Collection of the Royal Institute of British Architects.

hatched to suggest the lattice patterning of leaded lights, on Robert Smythson's design for a two-story bay window of about 1568–72 is more obvious. It has to do with realism and conveys very well the Elizabethan passion for glass used on a generous scale (fig. 5). Smythson and his architect son John (who died in 1634) made occasional use of color in their designs and drew a few of them with elements in perspective.

Throughout the seventeenth century, the greatest use of watercolor was for the coloring of prints and maps, both by professional colorers and by "the Gentry and Youths."[1] Architectural drawings were almost invariably drawn in pen and ink and rendered in black, brown, or gray. The reason lay in the influence of Italian draughtsmanship and in particular that of Andrea Palladio (1508–80). Palladio's drawings (brought to England from 1613 through 1615 by Inigo Jones) were all orthogonal and drawn in pen and wash. Jones continued the Palladian tradition for all except some of his designs for stage costumes, when he used pen and ink and watercolor. The tradition of drawing plans, elevations, and sections without color was continued by the second generation of Palladian architects, and it was not until the 1750s that both color and perspective became part of the architect's repertoire. In the late seventeenth and early eighteenth centuries, almost all orthography was colorless. Sir Christopher

7. Attributed to *Edward Stevens (c. 1744–75). Design for the interior decoration of a house,* c. *1763. Pen and watercolor (17⅛" × 25¼"). Drawings Collection of the Royal Institute of British Architects.*

Wren, Vanbrugh, and other English baroque architects almost invariably avoided both color and perspective; John Talman was the exception.

Talman, probably influenced by his long stay in Italy (from 1699), made or had made designs and many drawings of Italian buildings, monuments, altar pieces, and so on, that were "not black and white but every thing in proper Colors & beautifully Limned."[2] A set of drawings for a house near Hampton Court Palace, of about 1700, uses pen and watercolor realistically; particularly striking is the design offering alternative schemes of interior decoration—illusionistic fresco and stucco work with marble (or marble-ized) columns and cladding and a gilded ceiling are depicted. The cloudy sky shown beyond the windows is an example of realism, unusual in an architectural design of this date (fig. 6).

Elaborate and rather bizarre, Talman's design is restrained in its use of a full palette of color. Ordinarily, interiors of the Wren period have paneled walls painted in drab browns and ceilings painted white, following the convention that timber and plaster, for instance, should be painted in colors that resemble these materials. From the early eighteenth century, a preference for paneling of lighter colors, such as pale gray, stone, and white, emerged. The neo-Palladians preferred stucco or plaster walls that were usu-

8. Robert Adam (1728–92). Design for a Cieling [sic] for the Second Drawing Room at Apsley House *in London for 2nd Earl Bathurst, 1775. Pen with watercolor and gouache (16½″ × 23¾″). Sir John Soane's Museum.*

ally painted white; color was sometimes introduced with wallpaper and fabric hangings. From about the 1750s on, painted decoration became more colorful, since pigments used in house paints became more widely available and less costly. During the Middle Ages and the Renaissance, paints were prepared in the artist's studio or in the workshop with pigments (usually supplied in unrefined lumps) bought from the apothecary. Beginning in the mid-seventeenth century, color was prepared by the colorman (a new trade undertaken by artists), who also supplied the housepainter, at first with colors and by about 1730, with ready-mixed paints. The absolute necessity for architects to indicate to housepainters how the required tints of an inte-

rior scheme were to be mixed and where applied ensured that watercolor and gouache became essential parts of their drawing equipment; housepainters were familiar with the mineral ingredients of gouache and watercolor and knew how to mix colors to achieve an architect's desired effect. Thus a section showing the interior decoration of a house, of about 1763, is blue, pink, creamy yellow, and pale green, with lilac ornament on walls in the bedrooms, hall, and drawing room (fig. 7). A ceiling design by Robert Adam uses three kinds of green as well as pink and lilac (fig. 8).

A kind of revolution in English architectural draughtsmanship began in 1751 when William

9. Sir William Chambers (1723–96). Design for a mausoleum for H. R. H. Frederick, Prince of Wales, 1751. Pen and watercolor (19¼″ × 27½″). Sir John Soane's Museum.

Chambers (at that time in Rome) designed a mausoleum, uncharacteristically drawing it in perspective and placing it in a pictorial setting with sky, trees, and people.[3] This was due, perhaps, to the influence of his French drawing master, C. L. Clerisseau, as was the use of watercolor, instead of flat or graded washes, to convey the texture of masonry walls (fig. 9).

Sir William Chambers was a founding member of the Royal Academy of Art in 1768. One of its objects was an annual exhibition open to painters, sculptors, and architects; the architecture room has provided a useful index to changing tastes and techniques in architectural drawings ever since. Faced with the challenge of compet-

ing with painters, architects began to present large pictorial and colorful drawings. Considering, though, the increasing range of colors available in the late eighteenth and early nineteenth centuries, most architects kept to a restricted palette—warm tones of yellow ochre or raw umber, a clear Prussian blue, and gray washes were modulated with white areas to express masonry and sky. Incidental color was provided by trees, grass, and water. Bright accents were introduced with costumed figures that suggested scale and function and added pictorial interest to a drawing. Atmospheric skies—sunlit, cloudy, storm-torn, at sunset—gave great opportunity for expressiveness; landscape and townscape placed buildings in their proper location. These

10. *Joseph Michael Gandy (1771–1843). Design for a* New Senate House in St. James's Park *in London, c. 1834. Exhibited at the Royal Academy, 1835. Pencil, pen, and watercolor with white highlights (26⅝″ × 37⅛″). Drawings Collection of the Royal Institute of British Architects.*

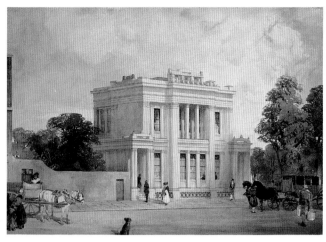

11. *Robert Lewis Roumieu (1814–77). Design for the Literary and Scientific Institution on Wellington Street in London, c. 1837. Pen, watercolor, gouache, and Chinese white (16⅜″ × 23⅞″). Drawings Collection of the Royal Institute of British Architects.*

"trimmings" might increasingly exploit the techniques of the flourishing school of English landscape watercolor, but watercolor *painting* could not (with rare exceptions) be used instead of tinted *drawing* for the buildings themselves. J. M. Gandy, the most brilliant perspective artist of the early nineteenth century, used watercolor over pencil (some of it ruled) and added diluted ink with pen and brush for his fantastic design for a new House of Parliament in 1834 or 1835. Painterly as his technique was, Gandy could not do without pencil and pen when describing architectural design (fig. 10).

Robert Lewis Roumieu's design of about 1837 for a Literary and Scientific Institution uses wa-

tercolor, gouache, and possibly Chinese white (patented in 1837) over pencil. The brightly painted figures may well have been added by another hand, for it is quite common to have an artist provide the entourage in architectural perspectives (fig. 11).

From about the mid-nineteenth century, architectural perspectivists explored the more brilliantly hued watercolors that became available (fig. 12). Although dry-cake colors were still used for the flat, transparent washes of working drawings, moist watercolors (introduced in the 1820s) and watercolors in collapsible metal tubes (introduced in 1841) were used for pen (or pencil) and watercolor perspectives with lo-

12. William Burges (1827–81). Detail of a perspective drawn by Axel Haig of a design for the Bishop's Throne in St. Finbar's Cathedral, Cork, 1877. Exhibited at the Royal Academy, 1877, and Paris International Exhibition, 1878. Pencil, pen, and watercolor (36³/₈" × 21¹/₈"). Drawings Collection of the Royal Institute of British Architects.

cal color and shadows. Colored inks were also used, but colored pencil, invented in 1835, was not much used until the 1890s. The three factors that worked against the use of color were personal taste, restrictive conditions imposed in architectural competitions, and the effect of architectural magazines.

The huge number of architectural competitions in the nineteenth and early twentieth centuries (sixty or seventy a year were not unusual) contributed to the suspicion that highly finished color drawings detracted from the merits of good designs executed without color. This led to a rule that allowed only gray or sepia washes in some of the most important competitions (for

example, the House of Parliament competition of 1835). Eventually (after 1903) perspectives too were more or less banned from competitions, though they were still made for exhibition and publication.

Architectural magazines that in 1868 (and in the United States, 1876) began using photolithography (which allowed pen drawings to be reproduced without being redrawn or engraved) had an even greater impact on the use of color. Architects naturally favored a medium suitable for the direct publication of their drawings, and in the 1870s and '80s, the architecture room at the Royal Academy saw a flowering of pen-and-ink perspectives.

13. Thomas Edward Collcutt (1841–1924). Contract drawing for the Imperial Institute in South Kensington, London, 1888. Pen and colored washes (39½" × 29¾"). Drawings Collection of the Royal Institute of British Architects.

As perspectives were becoming black and white (or sepia and white), however, working drawings were becoming more colorful. Color in an architectural drawing can be decorative; it can convey information about the use of color in or on a building; it can add realism and enhance pictorial values; and it can make a drawing more easy to read, for example, in distinguishing old and new work on a plan, or indicating function by identifying different building materials.

Colored washes that distinguish function, such as flues and drainpipes, can sometimes be found on eighteenth-century architectural drawings, but it was the engineers who, from the 1780s on, had the greatest need for colored drawings that differentiated the parts of an engine or the flows within a system.

The conventions of indicating masonry with a pink wash and timber with a yellow wash on a plan or section have been found on drawings of about 1671.[4] And from the beginning of the eighteenth century, two colors on a plan to indicate existing structures and additions to these are quite common: often gray is used for old work and pink or yellow for new. A floor plan of about 1765 uses gray for masonry, yellow for corbelled masonry support, brown and olive green to distinguish the different kinds of timber used for beams and joists.[5] Formal color coding to indicate different building materials became essential beginning in the 1850s and '60s when competitive tendering reached a new height and estimators needed as much information as possible.

R. Phené Spiers's book, *Architectural Draw-*

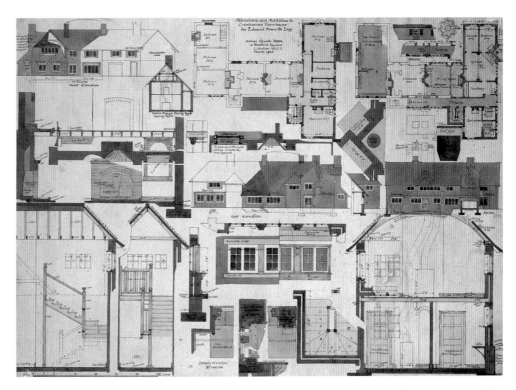

14. Halsey Ricardo (1854–1928). Working drawing for additions to Crimbourne Farm in Sussex, 1925. Pen and colored washes (22" × 30¹/₈"). Drawings Collection of the Royal Institute of British Architects.

ing, published in 1887, suggested that "the colors which seem to be generally accepted in most architects' offices" include Venetian or light red for brickwork, yellow ochre for unwrought firs and deals (wrought was represented by burnt sienna), warm sepia for oak, indigo for slate, mottled cobalt for glass, and so on. Spiers advised against bright carmine for sections of walls and Indian yellow for woodwork, describing them as "rather violent and crude when unmixed."[6] He could not have been happy when in the following year W. F. Stanley introduced liquid colors in bottles that were labeled Brick Section for carmine, Fir Timber for Indian yellow, as well as Stone, Concrete, Slate, Oak, and so on.[7] Although architects followed closely the conventions of color coding, some offices had distinctive variations and preferences and often produced working drawings of great

beauty. T. E. Collcutt's office assistant ignored Spiers's convention of using "Indian yellow, with an admixture of Indian red" for a copper-clad dome when coloring contract drawings in May 1888. He reversed the proportions and added streaks of green to create a realistic impression of verdigris (fig. 13). Halsey Ricardo's working drawing of 1925 (a typical though late example of an Arts and Crafts drawing) remains true to the conventions, but although mottled cobalt had been recommended for glass, he, like most architects, preferred to use cerulean blue and Pane's gray to distinguish the internal and external elevations of a window (fig. 14).

By the 1880s publishing no longer inhibited the making of colored perspectives. Halftone processes of reproduction had improved, and watercolor drawings could now be satisfactorily

19

15. *Cyril Arthur Farey (1888–1954).* Student *Design for a West End Club House, c. 1914. Exhibited at the Exhibition of British Architecture in Paris, 1914. Watercolor over pencil (17³⁄₈″ × 26³⁄₄″). Drawings Collection of the Royal Institute of British Architects.*

printed in architectural magazines; in 1893 *The Studio* began publishing color plates. At the same time many of the architects of the Arts and Crafts movement shared a prejudice against presentation drawings and drew them rarely or not at all.

A new influence on British and American architectural perspectivists was that of the Ecole des Beaux-Arts. During the early part of the nineteenth century, drawings made by students at the Beaux-Arts School in Paris had been made in monochrome pen and wash, until about 1845 when deep-toned, rich watercolor became the vogue. In the 1870s, a drier, more somber rendering style took over, and in the 1890s the formal, academic rendering of geometric drawings in pen and graded wash (particularly associated

with the Beaux-Arts) was de rigueur. Throughout most of the century, construction drawings had been colored and, of course, archaeological reconstruction and design drawings relating to the use of polychromatic decoration were highly colored.

Accurate drawing combined with a meticulously graded finish of gray and discreet color washes in the Beaux-Arts manner was adopted by Cyril Farey for a student design exhibited in 1914. Farey was to become the leading architectural perspectivist of the 1920s and 1930s. He brightened his palette with watercolor over a pencil framework and an occasional white highlight (fig. 15). He was rivaled only by William Walcot, who used every possible media to gain his distinctive effects: watercolor, gouache,

16. William Walcot (1874–1943). Conjectural reconstruction of the temple of Diana, Ephesus, 1923. Watercolor, gouache, black chalk, and gum arabic (34¼″ × 47⅝″). Drawings Collection of the Royal Institute of British Architects.

black chalk, gold paint, gum arabic, and so on. His richest colors and most impressionistic techniques were reserved for drawings of Ancient Egypt, Greece, and Rome that were as much fantasies as archaeological reconstructions—a world apart from the plans, sections, elevations, and axonometrics drawn with a hard pencil (or pen) on tracing paper that characterize works by architects of the Modern Movement in the 1930s and afterward (fig. 16).

Notes

1. R. D. Harley, *Artists' Pigments* (London: Butterworth, 1970), 17. Quoted from *Accademica Italica, the Publick School of Drawing, or the Gentleman's Accomplishment,* 1666.

2. Contemporary account quoted by H. M. Colvin, *A Biographical Dictionary of British Architects 1600–1840* (London: John Murray, 1978), 801.

3. Drawing attributed to Chambers in June 1986 by John Harris, curator, RIBA.

4. RIBA Drawings Collection. *Raynham Hall* in Norfolk by I. E . . . [sic].

5. RIBA Drawings Collection. *Plan of the Bedchamber Floor showing the situation of the Timbers as laid in the Walls* at Wormleybury country house by Robert Mylne.

6. R. Phené Spiers, *Architectural Drawing* (London: Cassell, 1887), 44.

7. William Ford Stanley, *Mathematical Drawing and Measuring Instruments* (London: E. & F. N. Spon, 1888), 310–11.

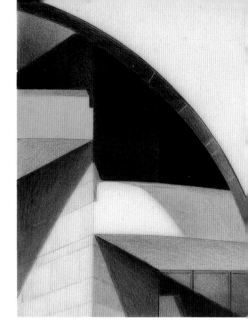

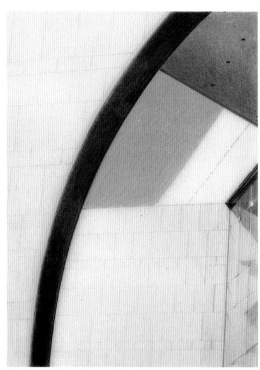

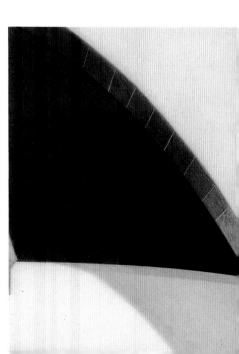

PART ONE: VISUAL AWARENESS

VISUAL AWARENESS
SEEING

Architectural illustration is a function of the artist's vision. The creation of images as the essence of illustration involves a process of specific and general communication. This process includes a unique relationship between the artist and the content of his or her work. The artist may begin by drawing what is visible, but he or she inevitably sees the subject abstractly or as a pattern of light, form, and space. Although reality in a rendering often incorporates a depiction of the "brick sample" and the "glass surface," the execution of detail is inadequate without the larger unifying elements of light, atmosphere, form, and space.

These qualities are evident in the works of John Weinrich, Hugh Ferriss, Robert E. Schwartz, J. Henderson Barr, and Helmut Jacoby and reflect a vision whose limitations lie beyond the facile execution of detail in reality. During the 1920s and '30s, when new technologies permitted the construction of skyscrapers, the notoriety gained from the publication of new building projects in newspapers and magazines greatly enhanced the reputations and numbers of commissions for many architectural illustrators.

The popular renderings of John Weinrich reflected powerful compositions using a limited palette commonly associated with the effects of diffuse lighting. One of his best-known illustrations shows the RCA building and captures the atmosphere of New York City; the subtle direction of light and shadow emphasizes the verticality of the structure (fig. 18). Hugh Ferriss, another prominent architect and renderer, was a dominant force in the field of rendering between 1930 and 1950. His publications, *Metropolis of Tomorrow* and *Power in Buildings*, as well as most of his renderings contain powerful contrasts executed with a charcoal crayon (fig. 19). Robert E. Schwartz is one of the most successful practitioners in tempera. Many of his techniques established a style that has been imitated since 1950 (fig. 20). The highly sensitive

18

19

18. *John Weinrich. Perspective of the RCA Building at Rockefeller Center, New York City. Pencil, pastel, and gouache on paper. (Photo courtesy of Rockefeller Center)*

19. *Hugh Ferriss. Chicago Tribune Building. Charcoal crayon. Hugh Ferriss Collection, Avery Architectural and Fine Arts Library, Columbia University.*

aerial delineation of the St. Louis Arch in figure 21 is but one of many skillful renderings by J. Henderson Barr; it reflects his love of detail and his ability to create a fully realized drawing. The highly decorative art of Helmut Jacoby is appealing not for its exacting detail but for his use of light and atmosphere to make a strong visual statement. His rendering of the Ford Foundation headquarters in New York City is representative of his work (fig. 22).

Learning to see requires exposure to visual stimuli. Becoming sensitive to our own powers of perception and developing an appreciation for the visions of other illustrators and artists will contribute to the development of a personal style. Learning to see also means being selective. We can focus on an object three feet or an object thirty feet away; however, it is not possible to see both objects in clear focus simultaneously. This kind of seeing is called *selective vision*. A photographer selects what is seen by shifting the focus of the camera lens. The illustrator, however, must create a reality by selecting a focal point within a given subject, thereby establishing a new three-dimensional reality.

20. Robert E. Schwartz. Proposed Oklahoma City Development. Tempera. (The Architectural League of New York)

21. J. Henderson Barr. Gateway Arch for the Jefferson National Expansion Memorial Competition, St. Louis, Missouri. Prismacolor rendering on illustration board. (Courtesy of J. Henderson Barr)

22. Helmut Jacoby. Ford Foundation headquarters, New York City. Ink and airbrush. (Courtesy of Helmut Jacoby and the Ford Foundation)

The impact of light and color on form within the normal viewing range of a real setting is also an important influence on the establishment of an illustrator's concept for a rendering. An evaluation of the color and value of elements that surround the point of focus can often suggest fresh approaches for depicting reality. Studying light and composition in the impressionistic paintings of Claude Monet, Paul Cézanne, Pierre Bonnard, Vincent Van Gogh, as well as the photographs of Ansel Adams and Alfred Stieglitz, holds abundant inspiration and influence in the development of concept and vision. There are no set rules or criteria for creating a successful illustration; however, a command of technical skills and facility with a chosen medium are essential. We will highlight many of the basic concepts of color vision throughout Part Two, including the elements of hue, value, and chroma. Despite a wide range of visual expressions and seemingly endless exceptions to every rule, a good illustration cannot exist without a vision and a plan for executing it (fig. 23).

23. Reality is captured by accurately depicting the effect of light on the brick tiles around the curved stadium.

VISUAL AWARENESS
ESTABLISHING THE CONCEPT

A good illustration is distinguished by one essential element, its concept. This is a plan, or matrix, for the interpretation of an abstract pattern of light and form and the establishment of an overall mood for an illustration. The concept and subject are separate elements that together constitute the essence of an illustration.

The concept sketch in figure 24 captures the essential elements of the final illustration with a few values or hues, a single focal point, major areas of light against dark, and hue accents. Creating a certain mood in an illustration requires study of the lighting level, the depth and placement of shade and shadow, and the effects of atmosphere. Because the concept sketch represents the structure upon which the final illustration is built, the flavor of the initial idea should be maintained through the execution of the illustration (fig. 25). One should avoid the temptation to elaborate on the concept sketch by adding too many values and color variations. It is inevitable that changes will occur as the drawing progresses, however, and it is common to stray from the concept sketch, overworking all areas in hope of achieving a masterpiece. It is usually best to trust the spontaneity of the sketch and adjust only the hue, value, and chroma as necessary. The choice of value, light, or color as it relates to the concept is inherent in the sketch and is the guiding force behind the development of an illustration. The mood suggested by an overcast day will be diminished by casting a strong ground shadow

24. Concept sketch.

25. Final illustration.

26. Strong ground shadows diminish the effect of atmosphere on an overcast day.

(fig. 26). A light-filled, high-key concept loses its effect with too many dark tones. A concept that is dominated by high-key colors requires value relationships that represent the lightest range of the value scale. The challenge of creating a low-key concept, that is, one having low or dark values throughout, is in maintaining this low-key look as details are added. Too high a value for the highlight on a window, or too many value differences across the surface of a building, contradicts the effect inherent in a low-key plan. To preserve the original concept of low-key value, it is advisable to use warm and cool colors within the predetermined range of low-key values, a range that determines the quality of light, color, or a particular atmosphere (figs. 27, 28).

27. A full value range with strong contrast of shadow creates the illusion of a pictorial space in full sunlight.

28. Soft light in an illustration is achieved when its deepest values are medium grays.

VISUAL AWARENESS
CHALLENGING ASSUMPTIONS

We often expect architectural illustrations to be accurate representations of reality; clients believe that illustrators practice a form of photographic realism. The creative illustrator grapples with these expectations, shaping or altering reality by the way he or she approaches a subject. An illustration of a building is often taken to be realistic when it is depicted in its "best light"; a bright, sunny day heightens form with strong contrasts (fig. 29). By washing the subject in a subdued morning or evening light, and by selecting an unexpected angle of view, however, a different, equally effective, mood can be ex-

29. Strong contrast in a full value range.

pressed (fig. 30). The viewer gains new insights that challenge familiar ways of seeing a building, and the illustration becomes interpretive rather than merely informative. The freedom to experiment with new and creative means of expression does not alter the nature of the illustrator's task—to use color, value, texture, form, and space to represent an aspect of reality, not merely to achieve drama. Figures 31–37 depict settings with particular views of their reality. The organization of surroundings reflects natural relationships.

30. Challenge the conventional depictions of a building by creatively exploring light, atmosphere, color, and value.

Conventional rules of composition would require a building to occupy the center of the illustration field. We have been conditioned to expect this. Interesting relationships gradually emerge and sometimes assert themselves with finality when we relax our beliefs and shift our position. Essential and creative elements of a subject can be uncovered by separating a subject from a distracting background, focusing in on a subject, or viewing a subject from above or from a distance (fig. 38).

31

31–34. The depiction of dress and attitude in human figures should reflect the building's function.

32

33

34

35

35–37. In any illustration, it is inappropriate to depict figures standing in exaggerated, modellike poses. Passive and active human poses should be illustrated naturally and in a manner appropriate to the function of the building.

36

37

38. *Focusing closely on a high-rise structure does not diminish the impact of its height.*

PART TWO: THE DIMENSIONS OF COLOR

Certain basic principles govern the successful use of color in illustration, though the application of color is highly subjective and variable. To recognize and control the differences in the three dimensions of color—hue, value, and chroma—it is necessary to know the effects of combining colors in composition. Color courses based on the teachings of Josef Albers in his text, *The Interaction of Color*, are readily available across the country and are worthwhile exercises for anticipating the visual effects of color relationships in composition. Practical experience with a variety of graphic media will also help establish an understanding of color mixing. The use of adjacent and complementary hues, and the mixing of single hues with neutrals and with gradations of values and intensities, are important exercises for attaining confidence and fine color judgment.

In architectural illustration, it is necessary to become familiar with linear and aerial perspective. As the term suggests, *aerial* perspective refers to the beautiful views from airplanes and tall buildings and the visual effects caused by distance and atmospheric conditions. Aerial, also called color, perspective usually relates to landscape and cityscape illustrations and will be discussed in greater detail in Part Three.

Many publications are available on the theory of color. Time spent with the study of color and its physical, visual, and psychological properties will provide a basis for creative and visually satisfying color illustrations. *Color Structure and Design* by Richard Ellinger is an excellent reference for discussion of color in composition. It includes many suggestions for structuring schemes with dominant and subordinate hues, values, and chroma. The discipline required to achieve an understanding of color, however, must combine theory and practice.

THE DIMENSIONS OF COLOR

HUE

Hue is the term used to name a color—the essential chromatic quality that distinguishes one color from another (blue from greenish-blue or green, for example). Hue also denotes the position of a specific color on the color wheel. In order to change a hue within a given range of color, we must mix it with another hue. When primary hues—red, yellow, and blue—are combined with one another, they become secondary hues—green, orange, and purple. The combination of primary and secondary hues forms tertiary, or earth-colored, hues.

The use of hues in architectural illustration, whether they are soft pastels or bright, saturated hues, has the power to inspire subtle reactions. The aim of color illustration is to represent form and space through the interplay of the color of light on local color. In figure 40, the ceiling is predominantly cool in hue, but changes occur around the atrium skylight structure that illustrate the effect of bounced light from warmer colors of the local building materials. We are able to perceive form because of the light reflected from it. The quality of a light source and the reflecting characteristics of surfaces and objects all contribute to differences in perception. The reaction of a viewer to an illustration can be strongly influenced by a careful selection of hues that predominate and establish major relationships among the various pictorial elements of the scene. Although red, orange, and yellow are associated with warmth and appear to advance toward the viewer, whereas blues and greens suggest coolness and seem to recede, a far more dynamic understanding of color temperature and push-pull space is demonstrated in studies of color relativity (fig. 41).

40. *Light reflected on transparent and opaque materials.*

41. A light background sky with graduated coloration in buildings.

A particular hue can be used to express coolness or warmth, depending on the way it is seen relative to other hues in the composition. A blue-green hue, for example, can be used to add warmth to a pure blue environment and coolness to a yellow-green environment. In figure 42, the color temperature of the yellow-green grass is deepened through the addition of blue in shadow areas. However, the deliberate exaggeration of the cool asphalt color in figure 43 is a foil for the warmer materials of the building. The application of tertiary hues and middle-range values would be useful to depict subdued or reflected light (figs. 44a, b). As a rule, any color is warmed by yellow and cooled by blue, but these effects can be modified by other colors in a composition.

The use of strong overall casts of a single hue in an illustration influences the colors of known objects to produce a wide variety of altered effects and an unexpected realism. A boldly colored subject against a neutral or subdued background becomes dramatically prominent (figs. 45–47). The roles of black, white, and gray values are therefore important in creating and establishing atmospheric effects and the mood of an illustration. Black, white, and gray values set hues within a desired value range and thereby establish light or the quality of illumination within the illustration.

42. *The color of sky and chapel roof are related to blue-green in the foreground.*

43. *The building as focal point through the contrast of warm against cool.*

*44a. The full play of tertiary hues and midrange values
in the courtyard.*

44b. Detail.

45. *Contrast through value control.*

46–47. A boldly colored subject against a neutral or sub-dued background becomes dramatically prominent.

47

THE DIMENSIONS OF COLOR
VALUE

A successful illustration is as much the result of value—the arrangement of light, middle, and dark tones—as it is of color. Value establishes the range necessary to create a particular light and mood of an illustration. Although we perceive color more readily than value, neither exists in isolation. A value study (fig. 48), especially in the case of a more complex subject, is the basis for the translation of color and its value equivalent into a plan for the accomplishment of a light-filled illustration (fig. 49).

48. *Value study.*

49. *Final illustration.*

There are many approaches to the use of values in illustration. Suggested applications include the selection of three values, five values, or as many as twenty or more, ranging from white to black. The selection of a high, middle, or low value range establishes the overall key, or mood, of the drawing (figs. 50a–d). The high-key range in figure 50a is associated with light values and atmospheric effects. The low-key range in figure 50c is associated with somber, ominous effects, and the middle key in figure 50b can contain elements of high and low keys in equilibrium or place emphasis on one or the other. The selection of one key is usually made to dominate and influence the largest geographic area of an illustration, with the choice of a subordinate key made to extend a full range of gray value into the remaining areas. The building of a full value range can occur gradually across the entire surface of a drawing to ensure the proper placement of values in a composition (see fig. 50d). Value represents the structure, establishes the light, and creates the atmosphere (figs. 51a–d).

It is also important to observe the differences between values in the subject and accurately interpret them into suitable grays or colors. The quantity of light observed in nature is approximately one thousand times brighter than the level of light reflected in a value range of pigments viewed in a typical studio environment. The approximate quantity of light reflected from a subject is determined by the selection of a primary ratio of values, commonly referred to as *value algebra*, and is interpreted to correspond to values in the context of reality. *Architectural Illustration: The Value Delineation Process* by Paul Stevenson Oles includes many useful studies of the relationships between observed light and form and their graphic representation. The selection and placement of the lightest and darkest values will generally establish a focus; all other values are then established to complete the range of light intended in the composition (figs. 52–54).

a   b   c   d

50. Value in color establishes the mood.

a   b   c   d

51. This figure includes a pattern of high-key, middle-key, low-key, and full-range values, also seen in color in figures 50a–d.

52. *Overall light-filled focus directs the eye everywhere.*

53. The desired effect in an illustration depends on its value range. A full value range with strong contrasts creates focus and sets the atmosphere.

54. *A pattern of light and dark contrast with greater focus in the foreground.*

THE DIMENSIONS OF COLOR
CHROMA

Chroma refers to the intensity, strength, or saturation of a color. The intensity of a hue can be reduced by its complementary. For example, the intensity of red at full brilliance can be weakened by adding green. Brilliant hues, however, are generally used only for special effect in an illustration.

It is important to control intensity of color, not only for the illustration of aerial perspective in a landscape, but as it relates to the effects of sunlight on building surfaces and in the resultant shade and shadow. Nature is full of bright and subtle colors; the rich, vibrant greens necessary to communicate an image of sunlit surroundings are therefore composed of analogous colors applied in patches and shapes that add depth and color perspective. In adjoining areas of foliage and shadow, it is particularly valuable to deepen color perspective by blending warmer hues of plant materials directly into cool blue-green hues of shadows and to eliminate the contrasting edge or boundary between their forms (fig. 55). The effect of a *lost edge* created in figure 56 by blending adjacent areas of secondary focus is also particularly effective in establishing color perspective without a significant loss in color intensity. It is possible to suggest movement toward or away from the light source by gradually changing the color of adjacent hues (fig. 57).

Throughout the year, intense colors are produced by the changing seasons. The leaves on trees change from yellows and yellow-greens in spring, to lush, deep greens in summer, and to intense yellows, oranges, and reds in fall. The colors of a landscape also change in intensity when seen through the moist atmosphere and regain their intensity in bright sunlight. It is important to restate a basic principle of mixing color: chroma can be changed without effecting a change in the value of a color. All concepts of mixing and color relativity become significant through their application in the illustration, which involves changes of hue, value, and chroma. Within landscapes or cityscapes, the careful balance of intensities of hues throughout a composition reinforces the value concept and therefore supports the illusion of light, atmosphere, and reality in an illustration (fig. 58).

55. Notice cool hues in foliage and ground cover.

56. Cool shaded areas in each study create secondary focus.

*57. The modulation of the intensity of a hue will suggest
movement toward or away from the light source.*

58. *Coordination of intensity of analogous hues in light and shade.*

PART THREE: ATMOSPHERIC COLOR

ATMOSPHERIC COLOR

ATMOSPHERE

Many illustrators use air and its effect on color to create and enhance depth and focus. The colors we see are always a combination of local color and all colors added or subtracted by atmosphere and environment. The use of light, cool tones in the background of an illustration gives an impression of objects receding into the atmosphere, creating depth (figs. 60, 61). An abrupt change in the haziness of forms from middle to background areas will create an impression of more moisture in the air, whereas a slower rate of change reflects the clarity of a bright sunny day. Illustrating everything in sharp focus diminishes the effect of atmospheric realism. Observing the way colors are affected by changes in the atmosphere throughout the year is important in order to convey a rich variety of color impressions.

The mood of an illustration can be greatly af-

60. Gradation in hue, value, and chroma.

61. The rate of gradation of color changes with desired focus.

fected by the studied use of cloud formations, or other atmospheric elements (fig. 62). Variations in the color and value of these elements define silhouettes of images at the focal point, or can be used to shift the viewer's eye across the picture. Although a few bright clouds may reflect sunlight, the background colors, values, and forms must be consistent with the intended color concept. The temperature of light from a sunset in a warm summer sky (or any other atmosphere) influences the remaining pictorial elements of an illustration.

Interior illustrations are subject to the same basic rules that apply to exterior atmospheric effects. Because the effect of air appears to lighten the darkest colors at a distance, details at a distance may require the use of a medium rather than a dark gray value. The foreground is always stronger and more vivid. It helps to visualize atmosphere if we relate it to the effect air has on distant objects. In order to establish the effect of atmosphere, the foreground and the background must work in contrast and gradation of color and value.

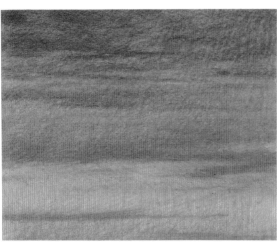

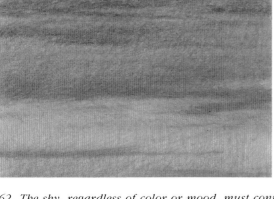

*62. The sky, regardless of color or mood, must convey
real qualities of atmosphere.*

63. A light and middle value range highlights details.

As one of the key elements for creating a mood with atmospheric effects, the background is of secondary focus and contributes to the look of the architecture—the primary focus. This relationship is often illustrated by using variations in the intensity of the same color in the foreground and the background, with the foreground always stronger and more vivid. The role of contrast to depict variations in the quantity of illumination within an illustration results in differences of perceived depth and detail. An awareness of light and the manner in which sunlight sometimes highlights detail in the distance and middle distance can channel eye movement across the picture (fig. 63). The placement of light and ground shadow throughout the composition should lead the viewer through the atmosphere and environment of the illustration (fig. 64).

64. The warm hue of the sky reflected in the building together with elongated shadows create a late afternoon scene.

ATMOSPHERIC COLOR

NATURAL LIGHT

Light is the most important component of architectural illustration. It defines the contour, form, texture, tone, and color of a subject. Natural light is so integral to our everyday lives that we accept changes in the quality of natural light without a second thought. Our eyes function very well in midday sun, deep shade, under a heavily overcast sky, and even in moonlight. An awareness of the effects of light in the environment includes an understanding of how various conditions of light change, and how these changes affect local color and its intensity.

Color within a naturally illuminated illustration will be affected by the color of the natural light and the way in which the form absorbs and reflects that light (fig. 65). As in the book cover illustration and figure 70, details can be enhanced by the subdued light of an overcast day; the reduced light blends colors, reducing the contrast of light and shade. Therefore, the task of illustrating "illuminated color" cannot be achieved by depicting color as it appears in a selected color swatch or material sample. Within the light-rendered surface, the actual color of a material or sample may appear, but the overall effect is the result of a colored surface or texture transformed by light and rendered in color-tone gradations.

Another consideration when coloring an illustration is the hardness and softness of light, which are subject to weather conditions and to the specific location of a subject in relation to the sun or another light source. Hard light is usually associated with direct illumination produced by the sun on a clear day. The subject will appear to have bright highlights and intense, clearly defined shadows. Soft or diffused light creates the appearance of an envelope of illumination, usually resulting from an overcast day or a large area of shade. In soft light, highlights may differ little from middle tones, and shadows are soft-edged or nonexistent.

65. *Shade on the building changes from warm to cool.*

66. An entrance in high contrast.

The direction from which light falls on a subject has a considerable effect on its appearance. Although the direction of sunlight cannot be changed, the subject can be viewed from an angle that produces the desired effect. The illustrator must also decide on the light of a particular time of day. Because the eye is always drawn toward light, the center of interest should be located in the light and generally at a point of high contrast (fig. 66). Greater contrasts of hue and value should occur at the focal point, with lesser contrasts further to the left and right margins. Spotlighting distant objects in selected areas through the use of contrasting values and chromatic highlighting enhances the sense of reality.

67. The coordination of all color within a limited palette.

Aspects of illumination beyond contrast created with shadow include fill light and reflected light. Fill light is general illumination, with the particular atmospheric conditions of a specific time and quality of daylight. These ephemeral conditions, such as the hazy glow of greenish light in moist suspension after a spring rain, can be captured only through careful mixing of local, atmospheric, and light-source colors (fig. 67).

68. Walls and ceiling show effects of light-temperature changes.

Reflected light is probably the most difficult light to perceive and illustrate effectively. Its gradient tones are responsible for the luminous effects of shade, which can change the underside of a viridian-green mass, seen as cerulean blue under direct light, to yellow ochre. The ceiling of a room with an adjacent natural light source is simultaneously affected by the cool exterior light, the reflected light of the floor surface, and the warm influence of artificial light in the interior (fig. 68).

69. The eye is drawn to areas of greatest contrast.

The use of chroma and contrast on the shady side of a building should remain subdued, so it does not draw attention from a sunlit surface. The representation of bright sunlight in an illustration attracts the viewer's attention and is where attention should always remain (fig. 69).

Shadow is the absence of light; it serves to anchor an object and illustrates the effects of light on form. The shadow is an essential element of composition, a useful tool to suggest the presence of an object that exists outside the limitations of a picture. Shadows contain the illusion of transparency. Shadows can influence the appearance of local color over a large portion of an illustration, such as the parking lot of cars in figure 70.

70. *The light is primary—the viewer should be aware of
the shade only as it defines the light.*

71. Gradation of light on the surface of the building.

The challenges involved in depicting the subtle nuances of light, shade, and shadow relate to the study of light and its visual impact on form. Practice and observation are necessary in order to establish the contour, texture, tone, and color of the rendering (figs. 71, 72).

72. *Nuances of light and temperature coordinate the building with the background tree.*

ATMOSPHERIC COLOR

ARTIFICIAL LIGHT

Illustrations created in artificial light differ in several important respects from those created in daylight. As we discussed in the previous section on natural light, the application of color in an illustration is related more to the reflective quality of light than to a color swatch or the local color. Light in interior illustration is, in fact, recognized only by its effect. The bright, cool-white glow of a fluorescent light valance will appear much different from that of a warm incandescent downlight. Using warm hues to represent the effects of an incandescent light, as in figure 73, creates the sense of a unifying and realistic light source. The re-creation of interior lighting generally involves warmer tones, both in modulating a particular hue and in developing shades and shadows. A large area filled with a single hue should be subtly modulated to create perspective depth, enhance the focus, and allow the value range to be keyed to the intensity of the whole illustration.

The color-value relationship is important for capturing interior light. Colors change in hue and value under varying temperatures and intensities of illumination and do not simply become grayer or whiter. Under strong levels of illumination, as in daylight entering through a skylight, red will approach orange, blue tends toward green, and violet appears bluer. Conversely, as these colors move into shadow, the hues shift toward violet or dark blue. The perception of daylight illumination and representation of bright light have great impact when we see color in highlights and shadows on the same surfaces (fig. 79). Effective in illustrations of interiors is the use of multidirectional light sources. Although such an exact depiction is difficult to achieve, shadows crossing on a floor is one way to manage it.

73. *The effect of warm light.*

74. Artificial light diminishes quickly.

The most observable difference between artificial and natural light is the length of their shadows. No matter how brilliant the artificial light may be, it is effective only for short distances and fades quickly (figs. 74, 75). This halo characteristic of artificial light is useful in the creation of the necessary focus of illumination in such interiors as a sports arena. The resultant shadows, no matter how dark, should always contain a feeling of light. An illustration that has light reaching all areas of the architectural space defines the space; the viewer's eye can be led across the drawing by varying the intensity of this light.

75. *No matter how brilliant artificial light may be, it is effective only for short distances.*

76. Cool light from the blue-violet sky contrasts with a warm incandescent glow.

Differences in the color of artificial light should be apparent when illustrating exterior night scenes, as in the cool fluorescent light of an office building, the warm incandescent light of an apartment or restaurant, and the colorful glow of neon and automobile lights (figs. 76, 77). Because there is no fill light from the sun, shadows appear stronger and objects close to the light appear brighter at night. Dark gray and black shadows, however ominous, should be avoided in favor of the dominant hues of night, such as deep blue and violet.

*77. Variations in the temperature of lights within build-
ings.*

78. *The coordination of ambient and store lighting.*

79. *Natural light dominates, and artificial lighting is a secondary source.*

80. Natural light dominates the warm interior.

The effects of interior lighting are established through an analysis of the space and an understanding of the desired mood. In figure 78, ambient and store lighting are fused into an overall luminous scheme of bright hues against a light and airy atmosphere. The interior of an office space should generally be well illuminated, with no dark shadows and with a high-key palette. The result is a depiction of a desired reality and the orchestration of one or more temperatures of illumination throughout the architectural space.

Many interior illustrations involve a combination of natural and artificial light. In these situations, the illustrator should establish a single dominant light source with secondary accents (fig. 79). In an atrium space, or one that involves a large area of glass, cool natural light should dominate and colors approximate objects in an exterior setting, with adjustments in the intensity of hue made to suggest the effects of tinted glazing (fig. 80). Color becomes more intense as the light spreads from its cool natural source into a warmer artificial setting.

PART FOUR: ENVIRONMENTAL COLOR

ENVIRONMENTAL COLOR

MONOCHROMATIC

Monochromatic refers to an illustration expressed in a single hue, with variations created only with changes in value. This technical definition of monochromatic can also be extended to include analogous hues that are perceived as a single hue (fig. 82).

In contrast with a conventional color illustration, a black-and-white illustration carries the viewer immediately into the realm of abstraction. It is through the translation of a subject into a value structure that its patterns, contrasts, textures, forms, and powerful or subtle variations in tone suggest a sense of color not actually present. Because black-and-white and monochromatic renderings are mainly created with different values, their subjects are altered and are therefore interpreted rather than merely recorded. The mood, atmosphere, and visual power present in a photograph by Alfred Stieglitz allow our imagination to see the nonexistent spectrum. Although the procedure for a monochromatic illustration is similar to that of a black-and-white drawing, the effect of a single hue is dependent on the use of low chroma. Tinted paper is useful as an aid in accomplishing this color concept because the hue of the paper allows for visual blending of similar hues.

82. Extending the range of one color.

ENVIRONMENTAL COLOR

METALLIC

The convincing illustration of metallic surfaces depends as much on the images and colors they reflect as on the color of the metal itself. Gold or brass is illustrated with hues of a yellow quality. Gray is used to capture the look of silver, chrome, and aluminum, whereas copper produces a reddish-brown hue. The unique aspect of illustrating metallic color is the surface depth created by the sheen of gold, silver, copper, bronze, aluminum, and stainless steel (fig. 83). Chrome, brass, polished stainless steel, and polished silver act as a mirror, reflecting all surrounding images. Because of the reflective nature of the metallic surface, a warm gray aluminum panel will appear blue in shade, as it reflects the sky on a sunny day, or orange, as it reflects the glow of the setting sun. The interplay between tone and hue is necessary for a realistic depiction of metal and its reflectivity. Photographic references are invaluable aids in duplicating the complex reflections in both curved and flat metallic surfaces (figs. 84a, b, 85a, b).

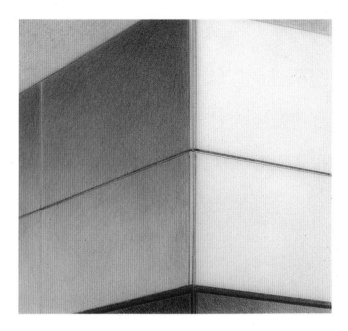

83. Reflective materials are affected by surrounding color.

84a. Reflective surfaces of glass and the drive-through
wall.

84b. Detail.

85a. Reflections in and around curved surfaces.

85b. Detail.

ENVIRONMENTAL COLOR

SEASONS

SPRING

The opportunities for using color and for depicting a light-filled, virtually transparent, landscape make illustrating a spring scene especially rewarding. Tree buds and blossoms appear suspended in space, unattached to their environment. It is a perfect setting in which to illustrate a building in its natural setting.

The growth that occurs in spring is generally best suggested with pale yellow-green as the dominant color (fig. 86). Blue-green is useful to extend the luminous quality of yellow-green.

Color and value studies will be helpful in establishing the picture tone necessary to convey the softness and airiness of the season (values in the middle range of the scale should represent the darkest level of contrast). A pink blossom will become white in the light and show the fullness of its color only in the shade (fig. 87). Selected areas of controlled contrast can move the viewer toward the focal point and enhance the quality of light (fig. 88). It is most important, however, to communicate the new colors and growth brought on by spring (figs. 89a–c).

86. New growth in spring is expressed with an analogous color scheme.

87. Detail of figure 68.

*88. Related levels of value contrast gradually shift
interest.*

89a. The mood and color of spring should communicate new color and growth.

89b. Detail.

89c. Detail.

111

SUMMER

The intense light of summer is its most commonly illustrated condition. The colors of nature are rich and vibrant, and the quantity of illumination creates strong contrasts between highlights, shades, and shadows. The atmosphere of summer is best depicted by introducing shadows from all the elements of entourage, including trees, clouds, and adjacent buildings (fig. 90). Because shadows are so prominent during summer, it is important to consider the relationship between the luminous color of shadows and that of the subject building. If the overall concept of the illustration is cool, vibration is created by the use of warm luminous shadows, and if the concept is warm, shadows should reflect cool hues. An extended luminous effect can be created with a cool hue at the edge of a warm shadow or a warm hue along the edge of a cool shadow, as it turns into the light. The perception of color is considered in relation to the effects of light on local color; strong light will diminish the intensity of color, although the addition of red, yellow, or orange to a light-struck surface enhances the illusion of direct sunlight in an illustration.

The depiction of the deep, rich greens of summer foliage presents a variety of unique color decisions. A cool, natural light creating an impression of green highlights is more realistically depicted with yellow-green and white rather than with pure yellow. In order to make natural warm greens representing grass more vibrant, patches of blue and red or violet can be used to modulate warm shadows (fig. 91). Both dark blue and deep red, rather than gray or black, will help create luminous, transparent shadows on background trees (fig. 92).

The mood of summer is evoked with warm tones; the selection of appropriate color should reflect this by mixing whites toward cream (for warmth) and by adding red and red-violet to the deepest shadows.

90. The rich interplay of light and shadow in summer.

*91. Summer is best depicted by using strong shadows;
bright sunlight is created with contrast.*

92. Shadows are best expressed in tertiary hues.

FALL

As shadows lengthen and light changes in intensity toward red, the rich greens of summer become the reds, oranges, and yellows of autumn, and new opportunities are presented to explore the effects of light and its nuances of hue, value, and chroma (fig. 93). The first hints of this color change are seen in the subtle shift from blue to violet-blue in the sky. It is important to observe these changes, as they are essential in capturing the look of a fall scene, and the color of light is the key to seasonal color effects (fig. 94).

The quality of light on a bright fall day can be captured with an increase in value contrast and with warm dark grays (fig. 95). The use of black should be avoided, because it will diminish the luminous glow found in fall colors. A convincing rendering of a fall scene is dependent on bright color. Warm dark gray added to the edges of forms will enhance the brilliant color of fall leaves, lend dimension to their forms, and capture the illusion of grayness that exists in the autumn scene (fig. 96). A misty fall scene can be created by limiting the darkest value to a medium warm gray.

Much like spring, autumn is brief and the intense color is fleeting. An illustration that captures the full impact of the fall includes the last fading greens of summer and the barren forms of winter. The use of a variety of tree specimens and the introduction of greens to enhance the brilliance of autumn's reds and yellows are also representative of this season (fig. 97).

The challenge of creating a fall scene, however, lies in the use of focus. By applying strong hues in the red-and-yellow range, focus can shift from the subject building to the landscape. Vivid color must be used only to set a particular mood and not to dominate or distract from the architecture.

93. Fall color is explored in secondary focus of entourage.

94. *The colors of the fall scene are expressed in the changing colors of the fall sky.*

95. Warm grays enhance colors in the fall scene.

96. *Warm grays in the primary focus of the building are coordinated with fall colors in areas of entourage.*

97. *The full impact of fall is captured in an illustration that includes the last fading greens of summer and the barren forms of winter.*

WINTER

Winter can best be illustrated with bare trees, snow, and warm clothing (figs. 98, 99). A photographic survey of a nearby park or golf course can provide an invaluable resource for various tree structures.

Although a bright, clear winter day with light-struck branches against an intense blue sky is appealing, the delicate pink tints in an evening winter sky are even more provocative. The changing angle of light compresses the amount of available daylight, so a winter afternoon can have the same appearance as a summer evening. In this light, the building and the trees or background elements will tend to soften, and the sky and distant landscape merge into a single hue.

Snow best illustrates winter with strong contrasts of color against whiteness. The effect of this intense light on snow is commonly illustrated in shades of blue with analogous hues used in areas of reflected light. Warmer violet hues that reflect sky color help to create the atmosphere surrounding a building.

Although the winter scene is most often used in depicting a "ski-lodge" setting, many opportunities exist in the light of the winter season to create illustrations of unusual atmosphere and interest. Many fine photographs are available in books that will help create convincing shadow shapes and forms.

98. A winter scene with cool shadows.

99. A winter scene with stark trees.

PORTFOLIO

In this postmodern era, we should not expect to have only one style of illustration or one synthesis of styles. Instead, we have as many variable means of expression as we have forms of life. The feeling is of an exciting new freedom and pluralism of ideas and not of a reactionary conservatism. Many illustrators are seeking to explore new modes of illustration through vivid coloration and pictorial imagination—the very essence of our dreams.

The portfolios that follow reflect a variety of vibrant new energies from contemporary practitioners of illustration and design. Each artist molds form and space to his or her own purposes, which are fiercely personal visions that fashion dreams, worlds, and populations to come. While their works are rich in technique and variation, each is tempered with individual compassion and a unique color vision.

Henry Matthews
Curator of Collections and Exhibitions
Muskegon Museum of Art
Muskegon, Michigan

Anthony Ames
Peter Cook
Harvey Ferrero
Christine Hawley
Ron Love
Gretchen Maricak
Syd Mead
Paul Stevenson Oles
Robert L. Sutton
James Wines
Lebbeus Woods

ANTHONY AMES

My drawings were conceived as a means of exploration during the design process. They have, however, unintentionally assumed an identity and life of their own, whether the project was realized or not. They have become autonomous—of and about themselves. The technique suggests an autonomy. The precision of the ink-line drawing suggests the precision of a drawing done by the machine (particularly in the age of computer drafting). Likewise, here the use of color overlay, in the form of a plastic film, manifests a process removed from the warm and sensitive touch of the artist's hand. Once the colors are selected, they can be applied by anyone, or by machine. Not unlike the modern-movement architecture of the machine age, the drawings allude to a technique and method of an age not yet arrived, but imminent.

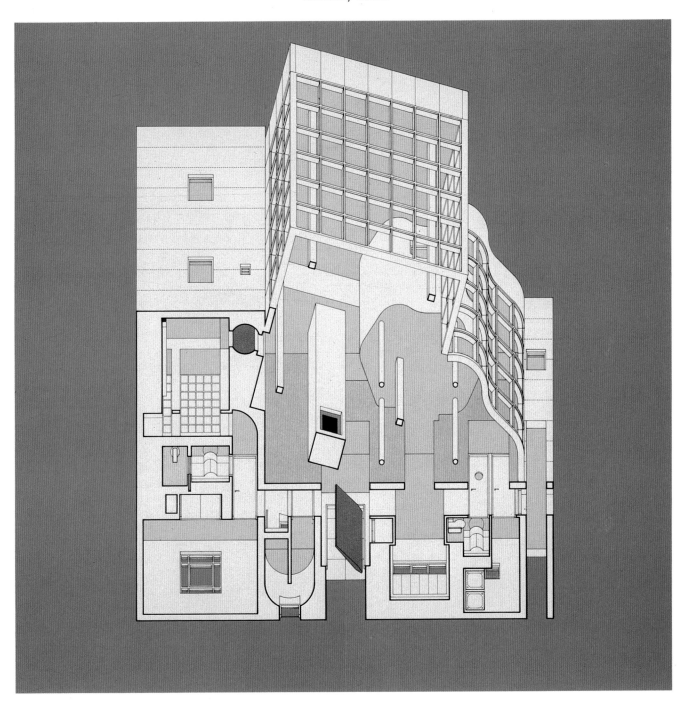

100. A Garden Pavilion, *axonometric drawing.*

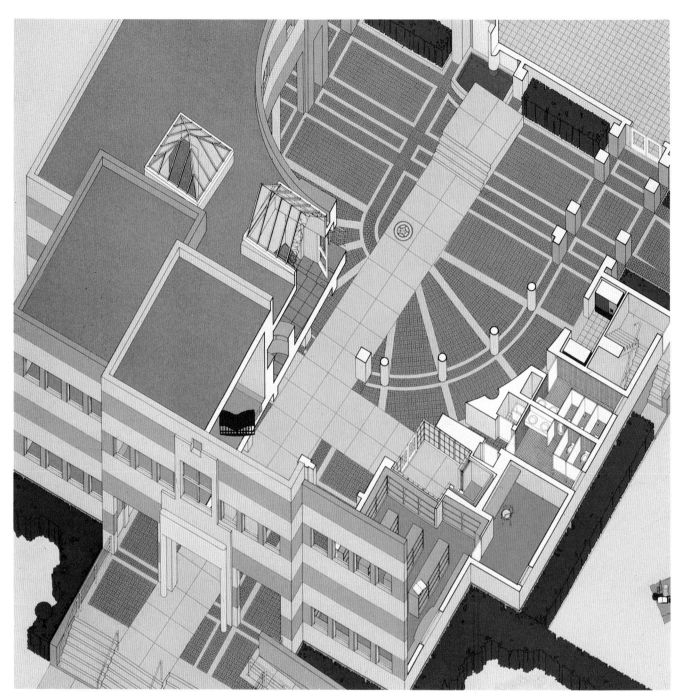

101. The Atlanta Botanical Garden, *bird's-eye cutaway section—axonometric.*

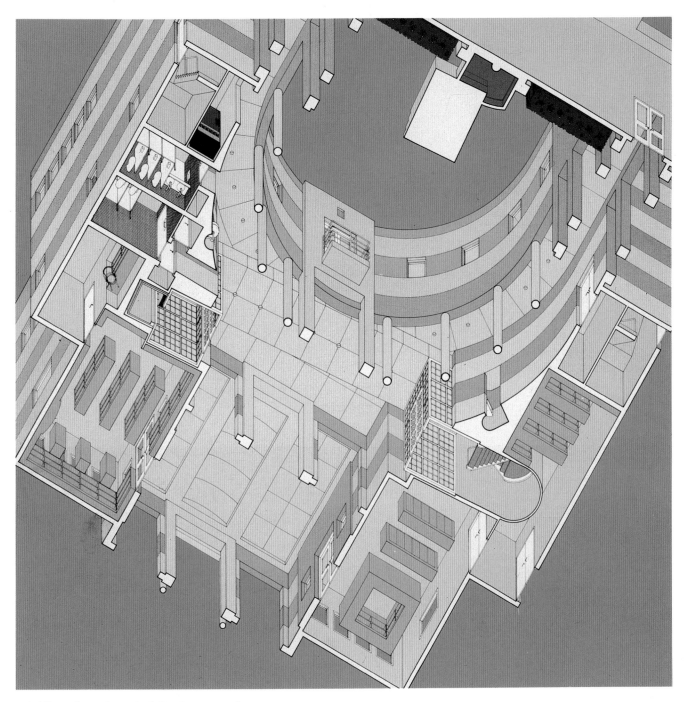

102. The Atlanta Botanical Garden, *worm's-eye axonometric drawing.*

103. Son of Chang, *axonometric drawing.*

104. Martinelli Residence, *bird's-eye cutaway—axono-metric drawing.*

PETER COOK AND CHRISTINE HAWLEY

Our use of and attitude toward color has developed in different ways. Peter Cook's drawings use color in an instrumental fashion—to codify, classify, or explain an ambiguous idea. The colors used in these illustrations are flat, dense, and usually primary; the intention is to produce an image that has a striking graphic composition with great visual impact.

The recent drawings by Christine Hawley are monochromatic. The media are often highly diluted and applied in layers to give the image a three-dimensional quality. The use of a limited palette in these drawings is as a tool that accentuates the figurative and builds atmospheric effect.

Our joint work attempts to combine techniques whenever appropriate.

105. Peter Cook. Real City "Tower," *1987. Crayon and airbrush.*

106. Peter Cook. Real City "Villa," *1986. Crayon and air-brush.*

107. *Christine Hawley.* Meshed Ground, *1978. Cartridge
paper, airbrush, and eye makeup.*

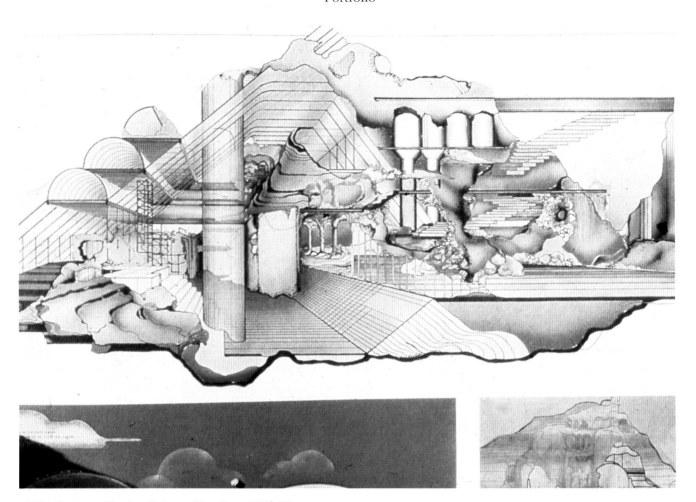

108. Christine Hawley. Brixton Housing, *1976. Photo-graphic print and airbrush.*

109. Peter Cook. Real City "Villa," 1987. Crayon and airbrush.

110. Christine Hawley. Superstar House, *1975. Black cartridge paper, wrapping paper, acetate, Rotring ink, tissue paper, airbrush, masking tape, and Pentel.*

146

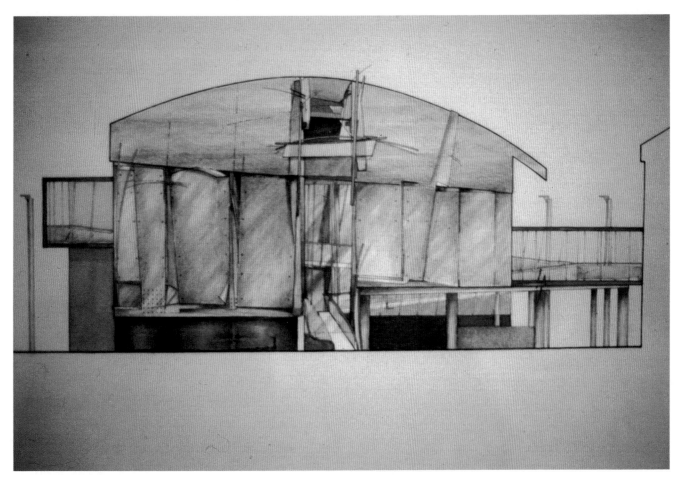

111. Peter Cook and Christine Hawley. Langen Museum,
1986. Cartridge paper, pencil, watercolor, and crayon.

HARVEY FERRERO AND GRETCHEN MARICAK

We have always been excited by the application of organic forms to architectural design and illustration. Our work concentrates on the principles of nature—in both design and composition—and evolves from piece to piece in much the same manner as elements in nature evolve.

Gretchen Maricak's illustration of a church, *Shrine to Gaudi,* employs a shaft of light to illuminate the interior of the transparent sanctuary and bring the viewer's eye to the core of the composition. Light reflects above the structure, where specters of Gaudi's great architectural accomplishments hover in a misty background. Her environment in *Tangerine Reverie,* a transfiguration of nature, is a metaphorical garden synonymous with new and unexpected manmade and natural forms.

As an alternative to current architectural thinking, Harvey Ferrero's work concerns the modulation of light, form, and the visual properties of materials. Parallel to the process of growth in nature, organic elements conceived in a state of change are characterized by the role of light in a visual dialogue of transparent, translucent, and reflective surfaces. The designs for the *Annie Oakley Museum* incorporate light reflected across the surface of a transparent tipi, while the image of a female figure emerges with reflected color from the interior space. *Transformations,* the four-part metamorphosis composition, begins on the left with a view of H. H. Richardson's Ames Building and evolves, through a transparent and translucent simplification of form, to a streamline masonry composition. Similarly, the vertical transformation in *Test-Tubes-R-Us* is designed with a cluster of opaque organic forms at the base, rising through translucent forms to transparent crystalline forms at the apex, which suggest the futuristic headquarters for a chemical company or similar corporate structure.

Drawing has always been at the core of our design process. It gives life to our thoughts and conveys our ideas about architecture to others.

112. *Harvey Ferrero*. Test-Tubes-R-Us. Wax pencil, pastel, and colored paper.

113. Gretchen Maricak. Shrine to Gaudi. *Wax pencil, pastel, and colored paper.*

114. Gretchen Maricak. Tangerine Reverie. *Airbrush.*

115. Harvey Ferrero. Annie Oakley Museum. *Wax pencil, pastel, and colored paper.*

116. Harvey Ferrero. Annie Oakley Museum. *Wax pencil, pastel, and colored paper.*

117. Harvey Ferrero. Transformations. *Airbrush, pencil, pastel, and colored papers.*

RON LOVE

Most of my work is "finished" rendering in full color. A few pieces are of the sketchlike variety. The reason for the emphasis on the former is client demand. What I attempt to do is to create a lively and pleasing aesthetic for a largely representational and commercial illustration. A careful value plan is a necessary first step toward the establishment of a lively and well-defined graphic pattern of lights and darks throughout a space. I apply color to subjects and use color to model surface textures and create nuances of light, which animate the basic value composition. Although I distinguish between the application of value and color when executing a rendering, I visualize each subject as a unified image; that is, I form at least one color vision of a subject in my mind before I separate and organize the graphic/illustrative processes that enable me to create it. The procedure for most of my work is as follows:

1. I select a point of view, mechanically constructing perspective on tracing paper (sometimes with the use of model photographs or computer projections).

2. A black-and-white value study organizes light patterns and composition (the most important step; it makes everything else work).

3. I transfer an image to illustration board (I use Crescent #110 or #1 Illustrator Board).

4. I create a value plan with a pen-and-ink drawing. The drawing illustrates desired effects, which might include the use of outline, hatching, stippling, and so on.

5. Finally, I apply color, including acrylics mixed with gel to create a simple color wash, overlays of pastel chalk, or Marshalls photo-tinting oil color. My more elaborate renderings are executed with a combination of watercolor, acrylic paint, and gouache, using sable brushes, ruling pens, and airbrush. I also use tapes, friskets, and liquid masks in most of my color renderings.

118. Condominium Apartment, *James K. M. Cheng, Architect, Vancouver, B.C., Canada.*

119. Apartment, *Marvin Meltzer, Architect, New York,*
New York.

120. Apartment, *Marvin Meltzer, Architect, New York, New York.*

121. Lonsdale Quay Market, *Hotson/Beaker Architects,*
Vancouver, B.C., Canada.

122. Eye Care Centre, Vancouver General Hospital, *Dalla-*
Lana Griffin Architects, Vancouver, B.C., Canada.

123. Apartment, *Marvin Meltzer, Architect, New York, New York.*

SYD MEAD

I attended the Art Center School in Los Angeles and earned a degree in Industrial Design. What I learned in school was the methodology behind the techniques I taught myself. This methodology enabled me to produce excellent drawings consistently and predictably.

I have always been fascinated with the notion of creating a window into a future world. As a student, drawing better meant an opportunity to make my particular vision more real. At present, I am usually hired to create an original image that represents an industry or an organization. My success has something to do with my position as an outsider—I'm unaware of what is *not* supposed to be done. My background in industrial design, however, gives me a knowledge of mechanical realism that enables me to make "fakes" for movies or of products.

One-third of my work today includes film and television projects, one-third, design work for outfitters (boats, planes, trains), and the remaining third, illustrations for advertising, architecture, and other industries. The following samples of my work are taken from projects created for film and advertising industries.

124. Bladerunner: Street Scene with Club Entrance

Bladerunner: Street Scene with Club Entrance

This shot has intense, mechanical detail over-laid onto realistic architectural exteriors, with vehicles providing scale. Color was used as a light source, and was quickly painted in first, using a 1-inch flat brush. Detail was then cut in with tones of the light source, and highlighting was added to indicate surface texture.

125. Bladerunner: Blue Streetcorner

Bladerunner: Blue Streetcorner

The hot yellow of the club entrance draws the viewer's attention. The blue screen and green light in the foreground offer a cold, inhospitable contrast. The wet street vertically extends all light sources and establishes mood. Again, color as light source was painted first, and detail was overlaid to complete the picture.

126. Family in Ruins

Family in Ruins

This sketch was painted rapidly with an underlay of peacock blue. Layers of dry-brush detail were then added to create the background cliffs and block shapes. The dry application produced most of the stone texture. Finally, the vehicle, people, and edges were added. Although the foreground ledge at the edge of the water is actually unfinished, the blue vertical brush strokes produce a surface that looks wet and reflective.

127. Future Marina

Future Marina

A magazine advertisement, this scene depicts an elaborate residential structure and marina in the early morning. The overall color is toward gray-pink. Sunset would be much more yellow. By using cold blue as the base, the color shifts from purple and pink to yellow-white. Because this is intended for a double-page spread, red is used for the jacket of the figure on the right and for the costume of the figure on the left. This leads the eye across the disruptive gutter of the magazine.

128. Space Club

Space Club

The client needed to suggest elaborate, high-style dining, featuring modular ride units, strolling surfaces, and the excitement of being in a "space city" within view of a stellar event. High-chroma areas were painted to replicate the light source, and details were added to retain the value separation between the light source and illuminated surfaces.

PAUL STEVENSON OLES

Color is a powerful and elusive aspect of the visual perception of our world. A generally accepted framework for a discussion of chromatic elements is the triad of *value* (darkness/lightness), *hue* (color name), and *saturation* (intensity or brightness). Pure color may be seen as comprising only the latter two elements, leaving value as the single element in the nonchromatic, or black-and-white, image. In my opinion, that image is the essence of any graphic description of physical form. A person may be color blind and still receive most of the information available in an image. We see a black-and-white photograph or watch an old movie and soon forget about the absence of color.

Value, I would argue, is the sine qua non—the "cake"—of the image, whereas color may be thought of as the icing. Accepting for a moment that value carries the message of form and color carries the "flavoring," it is understandable that I have adopted a technique of dividing the task of communicating the two. This procedure is similar to one used before the advent of color photography, and involves the tinting of a nonchromatic image. I refer to this process as "retrocolor."

By dividing the dauntingly complex task of making a full-color representational image into two discrete operations, I find that it is possible to concentrate more effectively on the separate issues of illustrating form, on the one hand, and adding flavor, on the other. Although the original black-and-white drawing may be used directly for subsequent application of color, my preferred approach is to photograph or otherwise replicate the value image and apply color to the reproduced print. This process has the advantages of leaving the black-and-white original intact as nonchromatic camera-ready copy, and providing the basis for investigating many alternative color options.

The print to be colored may be translucent (Photo Mylar, Xerox on vellum, or sepia print), allowing the application of color to either or both sides. My usual preference is for an opaque photographic paper that is dry or wet mounted to gator board or masonite. A few photographic papers, such as Luminos brand mural paper, have suitable tooth for the application of wax-base colored pencil. Most of these are satisfactory as well for other retrocolor media, such as markers, airbrush, or photographic oils. My usual preference is the wax-base pencil, because it provides the greatest degree of control if not always the greatest speed.

A major advantage of the retrocolor process (particularly with colored pencil) is that color can be easily modified or even removed, making it an extremely responsive and forgiving approach to drawing. A major disadvantage is that although it is effective for subtle or low-intensity color illustration, the presence of black or gray in some amount almost everywhere in the photograph makes it less effective for high-chroma images.

If a building has been designed with intense color as part of its visual statement, it is best to begin with a standard color drawing. This drawing can be produced, of course, with the usual visual array of chromatic media (wet, spray, marker, or dry), but my preference is again the wax-base pencil. Although I have been trained in watercolor (and still like to do topographical painting), I see transparent liquid media as too risky and unforgiving for commissioned drawings constrained by fixed deadlines.

I usually use wax-base pencils as a transparent medium (in the tradition of watercolor), creating whites by allowing the untouched board to show through. Of course, the use of a toned or black board or paper categorically changes this strategy, requiring the use of light and white pencils for tones lighter than the base. Applications to a nonwhite board improve speed and efficiency, but they require a different mind-set, since the simple correlation of pencil pressure to image darkness is discarded.

Color mixing or gradation when pencils are used transparently is usually achieved by the layering of hues. The dominant hue is typically applied to the fresh tooth of the board first, with the subtler hues (used as flavoring) applied subsequently. Each layer is smoothed or tuned separately, as it is applied. Since the difficulty of value and chromatic (as well as textural) tuning increases with the number of layers applied, I usually work with a maximum of three hues.

The functions of color in architectural drawing are many and varied. Included are a set of eight color drawings—five retrocolors and three color originals—each of which illustrates a particular color function.

For the purposes of comparison, nonchromatic (before retrocolor, or in black-and-white reproduction) versions of most of these drawings may be seen in my own book, *Drawing the Future,* which was published by Van Nostrand Reinhold in 1987.

129. Color as Enhancer

Color as Enhancer

This retrocolor drawing of I. M. Pei's Johnson & Johnson Headquarters uses color in very low-key fashion to match the overall intent of the illustration. The vignette format and the subtle application of color (to a building for which color is not particularly important) seem to complement each other. Note that the sky is inverted, becoming darker and bluer toward the horizon. This is particularly effective in a vignette format, which requires the lightening of value toward the edges.

130. Color as Definer

Color as Definer

This retrocolor drawing of Cesar Pelli's Cleveland Clinic also uses color in a simple, straightforward manner. An earth-tone building is sandwiched between blue sky and green grass. When color is removed from this illustration, the dimensional clarity of the adjacent building's reflected image in the glass of the clinic is lost. The reflected facade is in shade and is therefore defined as cool against the warm tones of the clinic facade in sunlight.

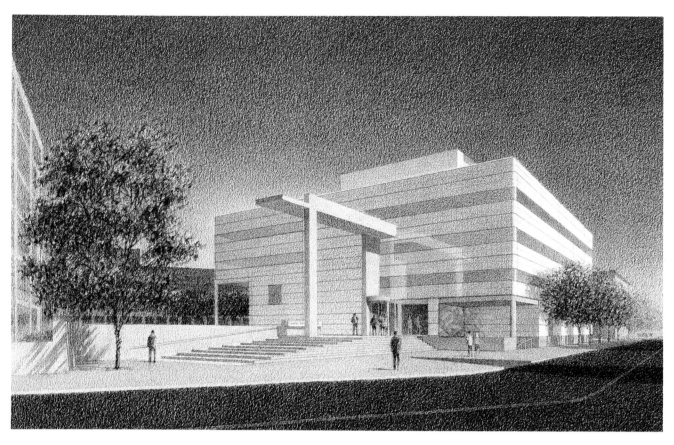

131. Color as Target

Color as Target

This retrocolor drawing of I. M. Pei's Weisner Building at the Massachusetts Institute of Technology illustrates how color can be used as a compositional device. The chromatically vivid mural near the entry returns the eye to the right-center of the composition in a manner not possible in the black-and-white version of this drawing. Note also the use of blue on the shade side of smooth, slightly reflective white metal panels. This results from the reflection of sky by hybrid material and is principally illuminated by diffuse, bluish sky light.

132. Color as Code

Color as Code

This retrocolor section-perspective drawing of Cambridge Seven Associates' Houston Design Center uses chromatic coding; the public sectors (for which the architect was responsible in detail) are depicted as *warm* and the proprietary sectors as *cool*. This simple distinction is achieved here through subtle hues on incidental surfaces, such as ceilings. Intense color is frequently used effectively as highly legible coding in transit systems, airports, and complex public buildings.

133. Color as Remedy

Color as Remedy

This retrocolor drawing of Araldo Cossutta's Cityplace Project in Dallas, Texas, illustrates how color application can rescue a flawed drawing. The sky in the original drawing was produced by airbrush, which allows no tuning. The blue pencil applied to the photographic print provided a means to smooth some irregular areas of sky value and introduced a consistent texture that improved the overall consistency and effectiveness of the drawing in its final form.

134. Color as Context

Color as Context

This original color drawing of Pietro Bel-
luschi's Miami Center Complex illustrates a
straightforward use of color. Whereas land-
locked buildings are surrounded by blue sky
and green grass (or gray asphalt), this waterside
complex (as viewed from offshore) is surrounded by blue. The expanse of blue sky
above the building and water below intensifies
the warmth of the earth-tone materials from
which the towers are constructed.

135. Color as Locator

Color as Locator

This color original drawing of TAC's mixed-use project, The Heritage, in Boston uses color to place the building in a specific site. Visual references to three landmark buildings and the public garden, and the use of red brick as the predominant material of the building, help suggest the location; this is clearly not San Francisco or Miami.

Color as Graphic

This original color drawing of I. M. Pei's design for the Library Square office tower in Los Angeles is a highly unusual color drawing for our office. It is not only very large (about five feet tall), but is executed directly as a nonperspective computer-generated line drawing. The intention here was to use color in a schematic, two-dimensional fashion to produce an intensely chromatic, powerful, and simple image. It is almost a poster, rather than a representational image of the structure.

136. Color as Graphic

175

ROBERT L. SUTTON

The wonderfully fluid drawings and paintings of Robert L. Sutton spanned commercial art, architectural delineation, and the fine arts. As a graduate of the Cincinnati Art Academy and member of the American Watercolor Society, he gathered a large clientele of prominent architectural firms throughout the Midwest. His works are in corporate and private collections and have been exhibited in numerous national exhibitions, such as the American Watercolor Society shows in New York City. His commissions have included Borden Corporation, Firestone Corporation, and Columbia Pictures. The following samples of his work demonstrate his superb control and delightful use of line and form. The elegance and supple manipulation of the vignette composition demonstrated in these and all of his works are seldom seen or matched in concept sketches and/or finished renderings by other contemporary illustrators. This portfolio sampling of his works is in commemoration of Robert L. Sutton.

137. Westwood Pharmaceuticals, Inc., *Giffels Associates, Inc., Southfield, Michigan.*

138. Commercial Facility, *Giffels Associates, Inc., South-field, Michigan.*

139. Texas Instruments, Inc., *Giffels Associates, Inc., Southfield, Michigan.*

140. Country Funeral, *Sheller-Globe Corporation, Superior Division, Lima, Ohio.*

141. Norman's Eton Street Station, *Brown & Lutz Development Company, Birmingham, Michigan, Roger Sherman Interiors, Architects, Dearborn, Michigan.*

JAMES WINES

My work as an architect deals with narrative content. Unlike most architects whose buildings are based on formalist principles, my ideas are drawn from social and psychological aspects of the contemporary environment. It is my belief that the ultimate function of architecture is communication as a public art.

As a narrative architect, it is my objective to find ways to create buildings, interiors, and spaces that reflect the constantly changing and unfolding drama of life today and to explore architectural language as a means of describing what Jung has called "the symbolism of the collective unconscious" or "mutable and evolutionary symbolism." This approach to the imagery of buildings seems more appropriate to a pluralistic world, one that can no longer rely on traditional, fixed symbols.

The fluidity, indeterminacy, and illusory qualities of watercolor have always seemed most adaptable to drawings that attempt to record buildings and capture their psychological effects on individuals. Because SITE's work often involves inversion, allusion, metaphor, humor, and the dialectic between apocalypse and utopia, it has been necessary for me to develop a free and abbreviated form of documentation—a graphic means to embrace both the literary and visual aspects of my intentions.

I also enjoy watercolor, because it is a medium that creates its own surprises—some inspiring new ideas that are independent of the subject being rendered—and because it can express mystery and evoke curiosity. My views of architecture have always involved humor and tragedy; only watercolor seems right to express this dichotomy.

142. The Paz Building, *1983–84.*

The Paz Building

The SITE concept was developed in response to the client's desire to have a converted building stand as a gateway project, symbolizing Williamsburg's dynamic state of renewal and its unique blend of cultures. Although the structure is to be used for commercial purposes, SITE felt that it should reflect the general spirit of the community. For example, such themes as old versus new, decay versus rebirth, wordly versus religious, and closed versus expansive seem to be more visually evident in Williamsburg than in any other New York neighborhood. A glass-and-steel tower will rise out of a fragmented contour accomplished from the removal of sections of an existing gymnasium wall, providing additional floorspace and a multilevel terrarium garden.

143. The Bedford House, *1982.*

144. Pershing Square, *1986–87.*

The Bedford House

This house was created for a private client in Bedford, New York, on a wooded five-and-three-quarter-acre site. Unlike SITE's commercial clients, the owner and his wife did not want a high-profile structure and, in point, had requested that the residence be integrated with the forest so completely that the final structure might become almost invisible. The clients also expressed a strong desire to "live with nature" and maintain total privacy. The final concept makes it difficult to discern where the house begins and where the forest stops when approaching the front of the building. This has been accomplished by allowing the forest to penetrate the architecture in several layers, and whenever possible, preserving existing trees and vegetation.

145. The Bedford House, *1982.*

146. Pershing Square, *1986–87*.

147. Pershing Square, *1986–87*.

Pershing Square

SITE's Pershing Square is a direct response to a first-stage opinion poll in a Los Angeles community. The message was, in short, Los Angeles wants "a *real* park, a park for the people." The people want shade, a lot of foliage, security, places to sit, eat, and meet friends, and no large buildings. The park should reflect the variety, spirit, independence, and creativity of residents of Los Angeles.

148. High-rise of Homes, *1981.*

High-rise of Homes

This project is an experimental multiple dwelling composed of fifteen to twenty stories to be located in a densely populated urban center. It is intended for mixed-income residents and will include both shopping and recreational facilities. The configuration of the structure is a steel-and-concrete matrix that supports a vertical community of private houses, clustered into distinct villagelike communities on each floor.

Every level is subdivided into platforms that can be purchased as separate real-estate parcels. A central elevator and mechanical core services the individual houses, gardens, and interior streets.

185

LEBBEUS WOODS

Invention and transformation are the aspects of architectural form that I explore in my drawings. These aspects best represent the spirit of our restless culture and suggest that only a dynamic architecture can express its underlying methods and goals. It is significant that nature itself evolves by similar means, indicating that architecture is meant to reflect the complex cyclic patterns and rhythms of nature.

The interplay of architecture, culture, and nature is dramatically affected by light, the subject of our most profound perceptions. The fantastic regions I describe in my drawings explore the presence of light, revealing its role in the creation of dynamic forms and their mutation through continuous experimentation. Color is a primary property of light and thus indispensable in my research.

149. Region M(7), 67

150. Region M(7), 61

151. Region M(7), 60

152. Region (A)E, 4

153. Region (A)E, 5

154. Region R(A), 5

155. Region (A)(2), 16

156. Region M(8), 10   *157. Region M(8), 9*

DESIGN CREDITS

Frontispiece Illustration. Smith, Hinchman & Grylls Associates, Inc. Detroit, Michigan

Fig. 23 Rossetti Associates/Architects Planners
Detroit, Michigan

Fig. 25 Nathan Levine & Associates, Inc.
Southfield, Michigan

Fig. 26 Smith, Hinchman & Grylls Associates, Inc.
Detroit, Michigan

Fig. 27 Cambridge Seven Associates, Inc.
Cambridge, Massachusetts

Fig. 28 Hellmuth, Obata & Kassabaum, P.C.
Washington, D.C.

Fig. 29 Cambridge Seven Associates, Inc.
Cambridge, Massachusetts

Fig. 30 WBTL Architects
New York, New York

Fig. 31 Smith, Hinchman & Grylls Associates, Inc.
Detroit, Michigan

Fig. 32 James P. Ryan Associates
Architects and Planners
Farmington Hills, Michigan

Fig. 34 Kober/Belluschi Associates
Architects and Planners
Chicago, Illinois

Fig. 35 WBTL Architects
New York, New York

Fig. 36 Rossetti Associates/Architects Planners
Detroit, Michigan

Fig. 37 Omniplan
Dallas, Texas

Fig. 38 Cambridge Seven Associates, Inc.
Cambridge, Massachusetts

Fig. 39 Schervish, Vogel, Merz, P.C.
Detroit, Michigan

Fig. 40 Kenneth Neumann/Robert Greager & Associates
Southfield, Michigan

Fig. 41 Cambridge Seven Associates, Inc.
Cambridge, Massachusetts

Fig. 42 TMP Associates
Bloomfield Hills, Michigan

Fig. 43 Gantt Huberman Architects
Charlotte, North Carolina

Fig. 44a Hellmuth, Obata & Kassabaum, P.C.
Washington, D.C.

Fig. 45 ADD Inc.
Cambridge, Massachusetts

Fig. 46 ADD Inc.
Cambridge, Massachusetts

Fig. 47 ADD Inc.
Cambridge, Massachusetts

Fig. 49 ADD Inc.
Cambridge, Massachusetts

Fig. 52 Kober/Belluschi, Associates
Architects and Planners
Chicago, Illinois

Fig. 53 Luckenbach/Zeigelman & Partners
Birmingham, Michigan

Fig. 54 James Stewart Polshek, and Partners, Architects
New York, New York
River Place Properties, Inc., Developer
Detroit, Michigan

Fig. 55 Sikes Jennings Kelly
Houston, Texas

Fig. 56 Hellmuth, Obata & Kassabaum, P.C.
Washington, D.C.

Fig. 57 Hellmuth, Obata & Kassabaum, P.C.
Washington, D.C.

Fig. 58 Schervish, Vogel, Merz, P.C.
Detroit, Michigan

Fig. 59 Skidmore Owings & Merrill
Architects/Engineers
Chicago, Illinois
Caldwell American Investments
Incorporated
Troy, Michigan

BIBLIOGRAPHY

Albers, Josef. *The Interaction of Color.* New Haven: Yale University Press, 1963.

Arnheim, Rudolph. *Art and Visual Perception.* Berkeley: University of California Press, 1974.

Birren, Faber. *Color, Form and Space.* New York: Reinhold Publishing Company, 1961.

Birren, Faber. *History of Color in Painting.* New York: Van Nostrand Reinhold Company, Inc., 1965.

Birren Faber. *Light, Color and Environment.* Rev. ed. New York: Van Nostrand Reinhold Company, Inc., 1982.

Bishop, Minor L. *Architectural Renderings by Winners of the Birch Burdette Long Memorial Prize.* New York: The Architectural League of New York, 1965.

Choate, Chris. *Architectural Presentation.* New York: Reinhold Publishing Company, 1961.

Duncan, Alastair. *American Art Deco.* New York: Harry N. Abrams, Inc., 1986.

Ellinger, Richard G. *Color Structure and Design.* New York: Van Nostrand Reinhold Company, Inc., 1980.

Ferriss, Hugh. *The Metropolis of Tomorrow.* New York: Ives Washburn, Publisher, 1929.

Gerritsen, Frans. *Theory and Practice of Color.* New York: Van Nostrand Reinhold Company, Inc., 1975.

Halse, Robert O. *Architectural Rendering.* New York: McGraw-Hill Book Company, 1972.

Jacoby, Helmut. *The New Techniques of Architectural Rendering.* New York: Praeger Publishers, 1971.

Lam, William M. C. *Perception and Lighting as Formgivers for Architecture.* New York: McGraw-Hill Book Company, 1977.

Lampugnani, Vittorio Magnago. *Architecture of the 20th Century in Drawings.* New York: Rizzoli International Publications, Inc., 1982.

Lever, Jill, and Margaret Richardson. *The Architect as Artist.* New York: Rizzoli International Publications, Inc., 1984.

Libby, William Charles. *Color and the Structural Sense.* Englewood Cliffs, NJ: Prentice-Hall, Inc., 1974.

Linton, Harold. *Color Model Environments: Color and Light in Three-Dimensional Design.* New York: Van Nostrand Reinhold Company, Inc., 1985.

Minnaert, M. *The Nature of Light and Color in the Open Air.* New York: Dover Publications, Inc., 1954.

Munsell, A. H. *A Grammar of Color.* New York: Van Nostrand Reinhold Company, Inc., 1969.

Munsell, A. H. *A Color Notation.* 12th ed. Baltimore: Munsell Color Company, 1972.

Myerscough-Walker, Raymond. *The Perspectivist.* London: Pitman, 1958.

Oles, Paul Stevenson. *Architectural Illustration: The Value Delineation Process.* New York: Van Nostrand Reinhold Company, Inc., 1979.

Oles, Paul Stevenson. *Drawing the Future.* New York: Van Nostrand Reinhold Company, Inc., 1987.

Porter, Tom. *Architectural Color: A Design Guide to Using Color on Buildings.* New York: Whitney Library of Design, 1985.

Sargeant, Walter. *The Enjoyment and Use of Color.* New York: Dover Publications, Inc., 1964.

Stamp, Gavin. *The Great Perspectivists.* New York: Rizzoli International Publications, Inc., 1982.

INDEX